TOCCATA

Suggested Registration:
Sw. 8. 4. 2. Mixtures
Gt. to 15th
Ch. 8. 4. 2. (+ mix.)
Ped. 16. 8. 4.
Sw. to Gt.
Sw. to Ch.
Sw. to Ped.
Gt. to Ped.

GEORGI MUSHEL

Duration 4½ minutes

The suggested registration is by Noel Rawsthorne who has recorded the piece on Ryemuse RP 7013 and ALR 1204.

OXFORD UNIVERSITY PRESS, MUSIC DEPARTMENT, GREAT CLARENDON STREET, OXFORD OX2 6DP